cartoon
KALI

cartoon KALI

POEMS FOR
DANGEROUS TIMES

jane
brunette

flamingseed
press

contents

1

*Copyright © 2017
by Jane Brunette.
All rights reserved.*

ISBN 978-0-9892605-3-4

*The poems "eyes of trees,"
"rat's nest," and "moss"
first appeared in* Eyedrum
Periodically, *July 2016*

BOOK DESIGN:
Jane Brunette

PUBLISHED BY:
Flamingseed Press

flamingseedpress.com

this dangerous moment

We've been breathing ourselves this whole time.

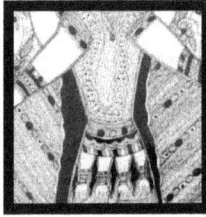

2

more flower than animal

*Gold belongs
in the broken places.*

introduction

Surely, the only
true revolution is
freeing the mind
from its own
conditioning.

—KRISHNAMURTI

A STONE MAY ALTER
THE COURSE OF A RIVER.

-Krishnamurti

on being
a stone. A few years ago, I had a vivid dream that

the world would end on a specific date, nine months away.
This might sound like a nightmare, but the effect on me was
just the opposite. In the middle of taking in this news, I had
an insight: if the world is ending — and all of human life
with it — I can't end social injustice or save the white dol-
phins from extinction. There's no time for any of us to reach
our so-called full potential. I might as well drop all my sto-
ries about what I need to do and all my earnest agendas for
what needs to happen in the world. There just isn't time for
that. If the world is ending, the only thing left to do is to
love and appreciate it while it's here.

I woke up from what should have been a nightmare with
a lightness and tender joy that lasted for days. I walked
down the road thinking, *This could be the last time I ever
do this.* The colors of the leaves turned vivid, people's faces
each so utterly distinct. Everything vibrated with fragile life.
Instead of leaving me in despair and nihilism, letting go of
all of my agendas for myself and for the world freed every-
thing to be as precious as it really is.

I vowed to continue living as though that date were real
— as though it were the last nine months of my life — but
I couldn't do it. The colors faded back to ordinary, and all
those nine months I noticed with painful clarity how my
agendas kept getting in the way, blocking my heart and my
clear seeing. As the date specified in the dream approached,
I found myself praying that when that day finally arrived,
the world as I knew it would end when all of my ideas about

"how things should be" vaporized in a fiery cosmic explosion — and everyone else's agendas burned up right along with mine.

In the years since this dream, if I'm to believe the news and social media, it seems that most everyone's agenda has gotten stronger rather than weaker. Opinions based on the flickering light of electronic screens are stated with such certainty that it seems everyone has become a fundamentalist something, certain they have the whole truth. In the face of this trend, my quest to loosen the hold of opinion and live instead from love and appreciation is a radical act.

All of this is to explain why I consider this collection of poems far more than apolitical, philosophical musings and personal reflections. While I never once mention racism or genocide or environmental destruction, every poem is a humble artifact birthed from heartbreak over the suffering of the world. This is what inspires me to dig underneath these symptoms in search of a fundamental cause or cure.

I've become convinced that the "cure" has something to do with listening deeply, and this is only possible when we commit to looking inside for our own bias and blindness before pointing the finger outside. I am not always so good at this, and so it seems to me that unplugging from the collective churning long enough to question my conditioning and deeply reflect on love and fear, the darkness hidden in my unconscious, the nature of self and of reality, is the most vital political action I can take at this time of heightened collective fear and insecurity. Such contemplation is not a replacement for engagement, but a cleansing of it. I don't want to add to that cauldron by speaking and acting from my own unexamined ignorance, blindness and survival instinct.

It is profoundly counter-cultural to withdraw even briefly from the matrix of busyness, distraction, argument, outrage and achievement in order to focus on such things, especially when the problems are so urgent. But our times are not special — the problems have always been urgent. Humans have always used anger or denial or a sense of urgency to cover over heartbreak and keep our focus on the enemy outside, forgoing the deeper work needed to finally do something different. This is why it's so important to step away from reactivity and attempt to see with clarity the conditioning we as a human family are operating in, so that we can finally stop passing on the thinking that creates such darkness to the next generation.

In times like these, such contemplation is the most urgent work of all, undertaken not as a way to withdraw from responsibility for the care of the world, but rather to increase the odds that every action we take is truly for the benefit of the whole. As Krishnamurti put it in the book *Social Responsibility*, "The prevention of this ever-increasing destruction and horror depends on each one of us [doing what it takes to free our mind from conditioning], not on any organization or planning, not on any ideology, not on the invention of greater instruments of destruction, not on any leader, but on each one of us. Do not think that wars cannot be stopped by so humble and lowly a beginning — a stone may alter the course of a river."

I would like to thank the whole world for helping me to write this book — and that includes you. Thank you for falling and getting up, falling and getting up. What else is there to celebrate?

Special thanks to Scott and Ashima for sharing their magical world high in the Himalayas, bringing roses and stone talismans, milk from the neighbor's cow and a depth of hospitality that was medicine to this wandering soul, such that I could bring this book close to its final form. A deep bow to all my Facebook friends who offered to read a draft of this book, especially Jillian Woodfield, Stacey Marvel, Mary Kay Cahill and Tesa Silvestre, who touched me with their careful reading and feedback on specific poems.

Finally, heartfelt, tender gratitude to my beloved spiritual friend and mentor, Kamalakar Mishra, who believed in me, and even on the night of his death sent me a blessing in the form of a dream. In the dream, as in his life, he showed me how to serve love in a heartbreaking world.

The image of Kali on the cover is traditional village art done as ink on paper by an anonymous female artist from Bihar, India, which I purchased at a small shop in Varanasi in 2001. I have often meditated in front of this Kali, finding profundity in the sense of this primordial, wrathful goddess as a friendly presence, a string of smiley faces around her neck in place of the usual severed heads.

I think of those smiley faces as the false masks we wear to deny and hide from our shadow selves, and the skirt of severed arms as all the actions we do out of ignorance and fear that create more problems, even when we think that we're "helping." Something about the drawing's cartoon quality encourages me to accept darkness and destruction as a necessary part of life and keeps me from taking myself too seriously, such that I end up another fundamentalist.

I hope that sharing my efforts at understanding and loving in the face of darkness encourages your own. It's become abundantly clear that none of us do this alone. After all, we're all brothers and sisters, sharing the same boat.

—Jane Brunette
Assisi, Italy, January 2017

By means of all
created things
without exception,
the divine assails us,
penetrates us
and molds us.
We imagine it as
distant and inaccesible,
whereas in fact,
we live steeped
in its burning layers.

—Pierre Teilhard de Chardin
The Divine Milieu

1

this dangerous moment

things born and dying,

in one gesture

bite the hand that grasps

everyone must leave
something behind

we leave ourselves everywhere
bits of shoe on sidewalk or footpath
strand of hair caught in a spider web
skin cells on the feet of a fly

was it the left pinky or the right
brushed that flower head
spreading seeds that otherwise
would have rotted in the next rain

even the man covered in tattoos
will one day shed his skin
bone unclothed and left behind

we've been breathing ourselves
this whole time

where war begins

andes mountains

a scorpion fell from the ceiling
landed on the table in front of me
elegant curve of pincers
in search of something to grasp

he watched me watching him
took cover under the candleholder
charlie had painted yellow
to resemble a sun-lit daisy

i don't kill insects as a rule
so it didn't occur to me
but once sarah recommended it
i had new thoughts

i could have put him outside
but there were horses   children   goats
he was a big one
and he waved his pincers like knives

so i smashed him flat
with a frying pan

this dangerous moment

life interrupts
the pattern of grey circles
that can form under anyone's feet

the underbelly of fear
a mad courage
in the tunnel of what is unknown

things born and dying
in one gesture
bite the hand that grasps

while a white moth
rests on only sky and air

knives fly through me

dark places are always at hand
steady knives at my ribs

yet they vanish like mirages
when i put face to the sun

the house of me
a stifling world

curtains and doors
shut out the breeze

until an absence
throws open the windows

and those knives fly through me
like sparrows or wind

eyes of trees

benevolent and stern
undisturbed by thunder
and the climbing squirrel
who springs and flies
legs splayed open in their boughs

such children
we reach not even to their knees

they see history
lost bees and viruses
polar bears confused
by dwindling ice and spring

the world melts beneath our feet
we stand on a thin plate of air
about to crack

pele's eyes
for linda

in pele's* eyes   green ocean forests
she sees with empty mirrors
that astonish   wilt all ideas of who i am

pele's face both bramble and rose
lips a carnation from someone's lapel
just married   passion contained

pele opens a fist and marigolds bloom
opens her mouth and chants fire
opens her legs   and a world is born

white peaks of mountains
where wise ones skate over glaciers
while down below   fast-moving glass

a turquoise river   sadhus clothed in ash
and in shiva's throat
pele's ocean churns with poison

*Goddess of fire who resides in a Hawaiian volcano.
This poem was prompted by a painting of Pele
by Linda Stephens.*

groan of shiva's bull   while pele
neck delicate   thin as air
burns ocean to earth   sky to sun

pele's fire mistaken for hell
but she is only birthing stars
the earth a blue marble

spinning in a child's hand

music in the fire

for middletown friends

somewhere else music plays
a bar in chicago
teenagers in a basement
a temple in india

somewhere else the drum
so fast   the dance
children hopping
sunday dresses flutter pink

but here

music in the breath
music in the heartbeat
and in the hiss of fire
clinging to the trees

where yesterday
i listened to the purr
of hummingbird wings

fire clings

i remember so little
of my childhood
so little of my learnings
so little of the news

just that it seems to repeat itself
while fire and the hiss of logs
could be anywhere

like the tongues of fire
in the icicles that hung
from my grandfather's roof

shimmering swords of angels
cracking in the morning light

shivering with my name

unsure if this is really my name
or if it belongs to a woman long dead

all those padded habits
roots of spirit burrowed into earth

play of shadow
like fire in the window

who says fire
can't go ash black and broken

who says thorns
can't lift the blackness

from the war inside

me as i am in a world as it is

indian himalayas

open now
this window painted shut
at the edge of my concealment

nothing to try or to achieve
when low graphite clouds
erase the mountain

as though it were still in bed
cushioned with pillows
a smudge in the sky

small bird trills a two-note song
i ought to sing
suspended over nothing

just light through green leaves
clinging to a stone wall
that holds up the universe

the agenda must be followed

for stacey

pencils sharpened   glitter box put away
we are here with a purpose and we know what it is
don't question the direction we're headed
don't remember the rust-colored robin
pecking at the earth in spring   seed of desire
after all   the agenda must be followed

law clerks dust the squeemishness
from their yellow tablets
prepare a crisp front for the judge
and everyone remembers to wear a hat
since rain is expected   a damp wind from the north
and we can't let the cold interfere
with the agenda   which must be followed

even when the frogs come out
for the first time in years
someone has mud on their boots
and we can hear the laughter of bees
in search of nectar
but that will have to wait
because the agenda must be followed

if only i knew where i put it
in this notebook or on that cellphone
maybe in an email
or was it scratched in pen
on napkin or notepad

the agenda   waterstained and weary
leaves its overcoat on the hall tree
and walks the downtown streets
in search of buskers
 trumpet player in the subway
saxophonist near the river

without an agenda
the sky opens its mouth and takes us
jonah in the whale's belly
at first we tremble
so used to the thick soup of time and agenda
sharpened pencils and the hum of gadgets
that drown out the sighing owls

to tremble is to live

for ken

like the boy
who couldn't shudder

so she slid
silver minnows
down his back

they flipped
inside his shirt

until
at last   a quiver

and i shake
the way shamans
and deer shake

shake off wax
left from candles
on altars to former selves

shake off old gods
who left footprints
on the narrow path to here

shake off the minnows
watch them gather
at my feet

writhing
silver light

morning news

they forgot to tell us
on the news this morning
that hope is deadly
the future never arrives

and this might be our last day

our turn to be the leaf
severed from the tree
rescued by wind
only to shrivel on the creek bed

what if it were in the news today
that there is no use in planning anything
we only have a minute left

and what could i do with one more minute

only listen to the wind in the trees
feel the air on my cheek
breathe in life
breathe out tenderness

when it meets the light inside
it disappears

andes mountains

in the walls of this house
are little holes here and there
you can see daylight through them

at night you can't see
the blackness pour in

but still the night enters
through gaps in the wood
big enough for a lady bug

full belly of the moon
on her shoulders

between beauty and despair

1
asleep in the church pew
woke to find my family gone

i saw only the knees of congregants
lined up for communion
the shoes on a pair of moving feet
polished and brown   my father

i slid from the pew   wrapped my arms
around the ankles that wore those shoes
nuzzled my cheek into smooth leather

smell of saddlesoap

knees flexed and a face peered down
not my father's face

2
the dandelions in the yard
how i picked them
hoping to bring to a jelly jar
the light of the sun on their soft heads

but instead they fell limp
over the jar's edge
faces sunken on the kitchen table

no wonder when my mother said
it was such a beautiful bouquet
i felt nothing but irritation

why does she insist on lying to me
as though i couldn't tell the difference
between beauty and despair

3
these days
i find my missing father
in the kind eyes of strangers

and keep flowers in a vase
until they bow down
drop their petals

reveal their naked bones

stones teach what my body knows

i took my legs for granted
walked numb over hills
until the endlessness
made me want to cover ground

so i ran
breath igniting joy
in the body that i forget

this stone wants to tell me
how water seeps through rock
brings light to hidden caverns
cleans dust between my toes

i have to sit as stone with stone
to understand its language
and learn to be unmovable
in my vow to breathe as love

this feeling i call heavy
not to be resisted
it is the ground beneath my feet
that withstands earthquakes

tundra wiki

the myth
that i could know
anything
about a tundra
from wikipedia

as though i'd felt
the sharp teeth
of the wind
as it bit
through marrow

and velvet sprouts
from hard ground
in late spring
sun bright
on cold skin

nothing exceeds like excess

for vicki of woodacre

she polished stones
gathered from the river
just to have them

days of sanding
until colors emerged
and joined the pile out back

she taught me to buy
a meaningless gift

pack of cards
a wooden whistle

then spend the whole day
creating wrappings
so elaborate

no one
would venture
to open them

just close your eyes

the partially blind
have the hardest time
she told me

if they can see shadows
they won't surrender
and be guided

they just keep
trying to see

if i weren't afraid of making a mistake

pack my blanket in a basket
with a box of crackers
not too sweet
bottle of merlot
chunk of pecorino

start walking without direction
no map   no ticket
no comb   no commas
no tea cup   no wifi
no apple pie

do more than wonder
what is down that back road

get lost in the chill dark forest
barefoot without a compass
soft rain
hollow tree
pine needles for a bed

hang from red velvet cords
in the theatre line
swing with the toddlers
until security
carries me away

we are walking through the fog with a pen light

grand canyon arizona

on the edge of the canyon
i walk for hours
stones plummet
stirred by my feet

i dream that i slip

instead of falling
i hover
feet alight
on ground made of wind

thoughts swarm like locusts
come to eat the sensible

forget anything you were ever told
by anyone but your own bones
and the pebbles that fall
in the canyon

we can bribe our demons

in the mud house above the river
it got cold that winter
so i used rapid breathing to warm me

but sometimes the cold entered anyway
through a door i forgot to lock

like those dreams i used to have
of the killer on the loose
and a house of flimsy doors

was he in
or was he out

i never know to stay or go
when the demon man
with silver knife fingernails
haunts me

but look how the light
glistens from his thumb

what if he will never leave
but only sleep
after a warm cup of tea

left for him on the porch
along with a rain coat
and a hundred-dollar bill

invite the angels
and a black-winged one follows

mudprints on suburban sidewalks
suburban illinois

mud puddle
at the entrance to the woods

too deep and too wide
i turn back   disappointed

halfway back
i remember

i could have left mudprints
on the bare concrete walkways

cutting grey lines
between crewcut lawns

mockingbird

vallejo california

a mockingbird moved in
i hear her each morning
and often in the dark of night

she warns me
not to repeat what others say
unless i make it my own

and the rhythm of those words
makes me want to climb a tree
and sing them to the moon

it sounds at times like madness

at ratu bagus' shaking ashram in bali

this ride changing
from tears of ecstasy
to dense gut
from lion girl to caged bird

she comes in from the back
dressed in white
as if for easter sunday
long skirt   prim jacket

hair in a bun
she quakes like a lady
does she ever let loose
not the dove   but the cat

you ride the tiger
or the tiger rides you

what they think of you
is none of your business
face the sky
outside the window

free this slave

forest church
indian himalayas

i pressed my thumbprint
into the bark
of an old cedar
in a himalayan forest

where minutes before
a leopard had gouged
scripture
with her claws

i won't be on the train

i'll be in the swamp
trying not to cut new channels
because people get lost doing that
go mad on their boats
paddling against the turmoil
that keeps carrots in the ground

it all looks so tranquil
but when the seed sprouts
the violence begins

that shoot we think so tender
thrusts its way up through the earth
with the force of a spear
in the unending charge
to get somewhere

when never have we left the here

even in this bog
sunlight through the cracked window
first rays of dawn

knife edge

borneo indonesia

the soft sharp knife
sits on the table
in the shaman's house

an old knife
he said he would give to me
the next time i came

leaf fades in a vase
flower turns brown
we age and we die

the soft sharp knife
bends like bamboo
cuts like a razor

dark creek

for patrick

dark creek meanders
through piles of merchandise
cardboard boxes built for shipping
the storage bins and warehouses
where we keep our possibilities

dark creek forgets its way
finds itself in a sewer
trace of wisteria
and rotting fruit
stale beer and a tawdry child

dark creek takes lives like so much silt
leaves them in dense piles
downstream from the bright city
where cab drivers dream
of a home left behind

dark creek pulls some under
while others float sturdy as rafts
sails catching the wind
all of them needed
to feed the willows

spin

bulls stop traffic
and the world keeps spinning

wars come back
like a skin condition

elephants throw tantrums
in mud puddles

and i circle the city
on the beltway

sure that i've passed this way
before

rat's nest

my house has been invaded
by the mad one
listless she wanders
from room to room

looking for something
she doesn't know what
it's always been missing
she doesn't know what

her confusion is what i most despise
the way she blends the edges of things
until the walls speak with white paint tongues

2
a rat dragged the legal pad
i used to figure things out
to the open space near the roof
chewed the edges as a snack
then tore my words into a nest to sleep in

even when i took the pad back
hid it under buddha's shrine
a few minutes later   i heard it rustle
the rat was back   insisting

if it were a dream   i could interpret it
but instead   the mad one
swallows a burning coal
the words meant to soothe
now a nest for the rat

3
is it possible to enjoy the hells
if i don't enter them completely
just stay in the silver space
where buddhas chant and om

the mad one
doesn't trust the buddhas
they are too remote and pure
she prefers jesus   dripping with blood
hammered to a dead tree

swearing at god

the mad one always feels better
after swearing at god

last night
she called him an asshole

holes to the sky

not on a grassy hill
but somewhere between
the time of caesar and tomorrow

someone peels potatoes
in a cave near rishikesh
while the yogi sleeps
beside shiva's fire

a beam of light
pours through the hole to the sky
lights up a staircase
carved out of rock

i walk that staircase to the top
where the tiny figure of a guru
on a tiger skin rug
sits alone with that beam of light

i leave him 100 rupees
as though he needs it

not on a grassy hill
not in a church basement
not in a hidden cave

but in the flowers that bloom
in the field near the ocean
under a silver sky

yellow mustard
planted in fallow soil
with the seed made famous
by the buddha

or was it jesus

all the same to me

forbidden medicine

yellowed photos of our ancestors
that bernard threw away

he didn't know their names

but it would have been enough to peer
into the grey imprint of a face
like the photo in my grandfather's trunk

man at a whiskey still
prohibition outlaw
getting away with something

this ancestor tells me

we need holy drunkenness
spawned from spirit and spirits
elixer and god

only one percent of mushrooms are edible
all others best left alone

we walk on air

sun squirms with shadows on the ground
i am but one of the fallen logs
moon without water
a mirrorless gaze

once   a crack formed
and the road opened like lips
a car fell in
eight feet under   slap of water

we walk on air
with only a thin film of concrete
between us
and a fall into grace

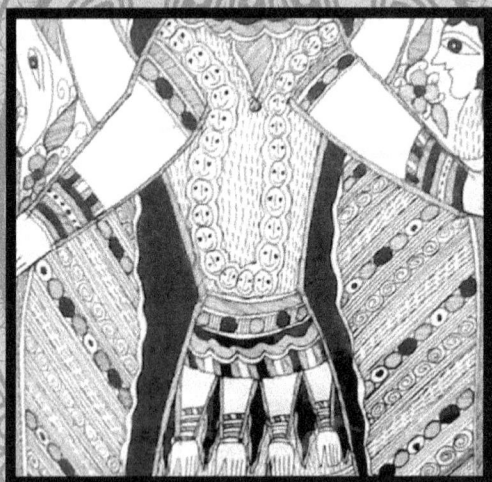

more flower
than animal

from a human skull

a flower blooms

scent of jasmine

kettle without a name

i don't remember my name
before i had a face
when other people strolled in shoes
out of fashion by the time i arrived

my name before i was given one
my mother spoke and it stuck to me
not the winds of my preference
i surrendered to what blew in

now thoughts surface like heavy fish
gravity pulls them under
then words appear
light as drizzle

in this faceless silence
a kettle boils water for tea

some questions

1
what is this life we fear
such that we build temple walls
and try to keep inside
the force that moves continents

we make a pet of god
the way we put trees inside pots
to make a pet of the earth

we make pets of each other
pretend to tame our wild edges

2
who interprets
the scripture of life

our inner fundamentalist
dark angel
white knight or peaceful nun
the wild one   the feral child

or the one who sits with hands folded
a stolen green apple in her pocket

3.
what if we played the hero
beyond the hero
the one not needing to be a hero
but a sigh

gold belongs
in the broken places

4
can we kiss now

more flower than animal

i lay my head
on a rock soft as a pillow
nuzzle into wet earth

a wild iris
happy under the rain's soft fingers
hair damp with the smell of life

out of a human skull
a flower blooms
scent of jasmine

we are really more flower
than animal

meant to huddle our feet
in the earth as we sway
surrendered to wind

with nothing to do
but let our fragrance
drift

mad saints and dogs

i fall in love with the mad saints
the ones who roll in the dust   ecstatic
the way my dog jakey did
when we walked through the forest

that one spot in the sunlight
he always stopped to roll
until finally one day
we did it together

he overjoyed
to have a disciple of dog play
shared rapture of powdered earth
warm stones and things decayed

kazoo

if you can hum   you can play
the package said
and so i claim
my ability to hum

first notes
like the drone
of tibetan chanting
so familiar in nepal

play it a little higher
and i'm a long horn
the kazoo
a pocket tibetan monestary

now the calliope in new orleans
cheerful and tawdry
carried from the riverfront
by the wind off the mississippi

this sound exists
but where can i find it
not in lips   memory
or molded plastic

to laugh like the hills

i used to think any bus would do
when i waited at the stop with my mother

a bus is a bus   all windows and seats
who cares what direction it goes

we'll end up somewhere   not here
and that is enough for me

why do hills and children laugh

for them   any bus will do

no one had ever held me that long

i was small enough to drape myself
over the neck of a yellow horse
and not be a burden to her
as she sniffed around the pasture

one advantage to being a child
lost in a crowd of children
they didn't know my cousin jackie
had lifted me to her back

and forgotten to take me down

i lay there grasping her mane
watching her eyelashes blink
dust swirl on her breath

i was the round end of her neckbone
a thick strand of her mane
no one had ever held me that long

and when i think of the girl in third grade
who kept a gerbil in her pocket
i know what it is to be that gerbil

riding against a benevolent being
as in the pocket of a kangaroo

the shock of being taken
from that horse
sudden chill on my belly
so exposed after thawing for hours
against her warm skin

no one had ever held me that long

how alarming
to have my edges back
a pat of butter now hard from the cold
wanting only to melt again

but butter can't melt itself
it depends on warm bread
the rays of the sun

these days
the dry hills of summer
are swathed in the color of longing
and in twilight's shadow become

the soft blonde back of a mare

sky on the mountain

indian himalayas

clouds start low in the valley
down there   the village breathes gray
up here   i taste pure blue
i watch that grey smoke rise
form white cotton balls in the sun

same clouds over red wisconsin barns
my feet on the rail of the fence
at aunt anita's dairy farm
where the white cow came to me
blinked her enormous eye
slower than i'd ever seen an eye blink
before or since

under that same sky
cows on the mountain
not white   but gold
gaze from their shed
blink away yesterday's dust
bones of their spines
visible through draping skin

benefits of aging

a more subtle world
free of distracting din

novelty loses its power
the familiar greying us

until the texture of sunlight
a faucet's drip   sky and earth

swing open their gates
and we can hear the grass sing again

like when we were children
or angels

or caterpillars

rock loves water
fire loves earth

rock loves water
water loves rock
they admire
each other's genius

water mimics rock
turns to ice
rock mimics water
turns to sand

for love of fire
i turn to steam
steam longs
for solid ground

rock asks
for my feet
in marriage

all the same stillness
ubud, bali

in the balinese guesthouse
curtains still closed
i see the rooster with my ears
his anthem struts through the stillness

i can still hear
that house we rented near the lake
where mourning doves sung laments
wings fluffed against the chill

and those moonless andes nights
broken open by the donkey's bray
sodden with heartbreak so raw
who wouldn't want to stroke his mane

everything held by stillness
the music depends on it
sky and poplar are one
leaves only sing if the wind agrees

wind blows through me

wind blows through me
where did i go
nothing to see here

just breath
in the flute made of smoke

a fresh current
takes me to a different shore
not of my choice

wind blows the current
wind decides

afternoon gargle

someone left mouthwash
on the bathroom sink
sticky half-round remnants
blue as afternoon sky

smell of fake peppermint

isn't it just like the madness we are
to use a plastic bottle
of imitation mint
when the real thing grows fragrant

just outside the back door

moss

i see a dead baby chick
still round like the egg
but with wings
floating down the canal

it might be something from a tree
but my mind makes it a stillborn bird
face down and drown

meanwhile
moss grows an emerald carpet
on the yielding bark
of a redwood stump

feed the birds

i have not fed the birds
the way that tall man did
doves on his shoulders
squirrels on his shoes

he emerged for only this purpose
from the narrow house
in need of paint
yellowed shades
drawn over the windows

now the tall man is gone
and in his place
scattered remnants
of seed   wings
and song

soul tech

i resist becoming a cyborg
human-scale tech
suddenly endangered

like sewing needles
spools of thread

i carry them with me
as i wander
darn my clothes
one stitch at a time

sew little journals
from local paper
i have a pile of such notebooks
no spirals or plastic coating

small things
crafted with human fingers

someone
needs to remember

listen to what is

that thing missing
i thought needed
before i could relax

it never comes

time to renounce
listening for what isn't
and listen instead
to what is

distant chainsaw
a cicada
gasp of wind
a falling tree

goodbye cement

cement stifles the earth
with our hunger
until it cracks
from a single blade of grass
yearning for the light

goodbye cement
you thought you were so strong
but there is less than an inch of you
just a scab on the flesh of the earth
helpless against buried longing

we want to eat life
naked and unchained
until we have lost all knowing
just the leap into something
we can't recognize as our own

time for something else

for tesa

traveler of consciousness
rest in this moment

set down your luggage
in this place of now

go slow   they tell me   slow
feel deeply each turn of your head

some things can only be seen
with eyes that rest as they look

when we laugh together

for hunter

the crying comes disguised
but made presentable

someone puts their foot in the door
so that everything stays possible

something goes soft
and something shrinks down
the mouse in its hole

the bird of paradise hides its wings
from the headlamp of a traveler
in search of wonders

still we laugh

over sleep and yearning
pretense and honesty
the broken heart
and the open heart

the kind of laughter
that prods the serpent
to grow feathers

the end of light and dark

thunder in the night
a bomb at the edge of sorrow
those caged spirits
now released
to feed the lillies

okay to mourn
to feel the disarray
not as something to change
but as something already changing
on its own

why rush it along
as though one moment holds the beauty
a woman photographed at just the right angle
just the right age
pretending a tulip will never fade

i'm a cloud that makes its shape
then remakes itself into nothing
touching everything at once
worshipping space

until space becomes a breeze
to kiss my cheek

the more i lose
the more i have

the more i lose
the more i have
the more i love
and the more i see

out there
people think more
but in here
i know the secret of less

when the lights go out
the electricity dies
the music stops

then the sky opens
and licks me
with its wet tongue

then the grasshopper speaks

there are doors in this forest
only the body knows where

limits

we are made
of our limits

sturdy walls
for the playpen

good that a rooster
is a rooster for now

hunger for something
that can't be consumed

for satya

we are born into love
or we wouldn't have survived
held in a womb
outside the womb

hunger to know
the gift of that
the benevolence that birthed us
diapered us

even through the terror
of not knowing
since none of us knows
what is happening here

rest in the love undeniable
pouring through cracked human vessels
we want to bathe
even in its shallow stream

the story of everyone

my sin
i pretended

their sin
they believed me

end of story
stop pretending

cure for breakfast blues

i could thank everyone
or no one
and that would change
how i feel about my day

thank you
whoever first invented walls
and those who know
how to put them up

i don't know how to build walls
and yet i've had them all my life
they are handy for keeping
crickets off the table

i could thank the crickets
for last night's symphony
and ears for the means
to hear them

the refrigerator is working
the hum tells me
i could again thank my ears
for delivering this news

i could thank the inventor of bread
(who passed on the recipe)
and the egg who hatched the chicken
who laid the egg

thank you for breakfast

i could thank time and space
for this opportunity
to sit in a wooden chair
(thank you carpenter)

which used to be lumber
(thank you saw)
which used to be a tree
(thank you sunlight

and dirt and a seed
and the navel of the branch
that had to let go
so the seed could fall

and grow into the tree
that dropped the seed)

thanks

not words

unsaidness rises
from its prone position

frozen face in the carpet
losing urgency   losing will

this is not bad news

something else
buoys the churning heart

sweet time

i take my sweet time
ripened like a peach on the tree
now warm in my hand
with morning sun

expedient time
picks the peach green
to store in a dark bushel
ripen in a paper bag

a crack
and the tree branch dangles
five or fifty years
until wind or heavy rain

drops it to the forest floor

swaddled

yellowed newspaper
cushions old china
speaks to the one
who unwraps it

of the time and territory
of the one who wrapped

sunday sales
and politicians
someone robbed
and someone loved

when newspapers disappear
what will cradle
the fragile remnants
of our past

children know better

as a child
i preferred plastic blocks
to the fancy doll
they thought i should want

too uninitiated
to see the distinction
between sunlight and glitter
elevator and ascension

under the mask of fear or culture
we sit as children
watching for the first star

simple quivering humans
astounded by the mystery
some say can be explained

small gestures

suburban illinois

i slept in the gazebo
hum of the neighbor's generator
masking wind in the pines

no one in the neighborhood
likely knew what the night said
so i listened to the earth breathe

in that suburban yard
between houses filled
with small gestures

gifts from the ones
whose culture leaves no space
for old selves to collapse

until black flies ripen and fall
filling a blue offering bowl
with translucent wings

poetry wins

in the belly
of my deepest desire
poetry wins

and that black-striped caterpillar
with a billion suction feet
now climbing the leaf

is far more interesting
to the average person
than celebrity gossip

sadhus

instead of going in
he went out
had to beg sometimes
steadfast hunger
until something let go
and instead of going home
or finding home
he was home
without walls or doors
keys or pillows

instead of going out
i went in
to the home inside
where fresh air blows luminous
over bleached white cotton
fluttering on a clothesline
old threadbare sheets
soft with washing

this
instead of the fallen leaves
of childhood
as summer turned
and the trees dropped their barriers
showed us their bones

now transparent to the sky
now the drawn lines
of a calligrapher

right now

i have a body again
with cells lonely for darkness
crunch of leaves underfoot
smell of last year's fallen ones

on the other side of the planet
people sleep in forest groves
while here
some wait for the bell to ring
others for the phone
or the penny   or the light to change

without knowing where to go next
sunlight and shadow lead the way
to where a monk chants in vietnamese
though my ears can't hear
from this far away

he may be in a tiny room in queens
or in the hills of vietnam
on a walk through green fields
warmed by the sun
suddenly free of role

the narrow wide road to nowhere

we omit the long dormant times
when we write a story or tell one

we omit years of gestation
and speak only of crossroads

the broken cocoon

why so narrow do we define our riches
when the path itself is life

after the turning point
we just walk the next length

of the narrow wide road to nowhere

no longer forgetting our origins
in the wide open mouth
of a baby bird

about the author

Jane Brunette teaches and writes about meditation, spirituality and creating a soulful life in challenging times. She created Writing from the Soul, an approach to writing that has sprouted groups around the world, and she mentors individuals in writing and spiritual practice. Trained as a psychotherapist and Buddhist teacher with a deep affinity for Christian mysticism and indigenous perspectives, she travels widely to challenge her social conditioning, living simply in cultures where this is still possible to free her time and her mind for contemplation and retreat. This book and her first book of poetry, *Grasshopper Guru,* both emerged from a long cycle of solitary retreat and pilgrimage. Her websites are writingfromthesoul.net and flamingseed.com.

.

**Writing
from the
SOUL**

Many of the poems in this book
began as freewrites
in Writing from the Soul circles
with friends and clients.
Big thanks to all of the writers
who have played with me in this way.
I hope this book inspires you
to make one of your own.

Jane Brunette
writingfromthesoul.net